Dear GOD, How did I get here?

CRYSTAL HICKS

Crystal Hicks

Copyright © 2019 by Crystal Hicks
All rights reserved. In accordance with the U.S. Copyright Act of 1976, the scanning, uploading, and electronic sharing of any part of this book without the permission of the publisher constitute unlawful piracy and theft of the author's intellectual property. If you would like to use material from the book (other than for review purposes), prior written permission must be obtained by contacting the publisher New Wineskin Int'l Ministry, LLC at NWIMLLC@GMAIL.COM
Library of Congress Publication Data
Crystal Hicks
Dear GOD How Did I Get Here?

ISBN-13: 978-1-64483-004-8
ISBN-10: 1-64483-004-3

Acknowledgment

Crystal Hicks is a powerful woman of God. Her journey has been rough and tumbled. I was engrossed in how God was always faithful to lift her out of her circumstances. You will be astounded by how God continually rescued her and put her back on the path so she could carry on her journey with Him. "Dear God" is written from the heart and experiences of Crystal Hicks. Each of us is created as unique individuals in God's eye. Therefore, we all have different life experiences resulting in unique emotional, spiritual and physical wounds. God wants to heal those wounds so you can complete His purposes in your life. How do we get healed when we are so broken and wounded? God is giving us a jump-off point through Crystal's testimony of her healing. If you take the time to examine your life in the parameters she has set forth within these pages, you can create your testimony, and you will begin your journey.

Carol Basile
Destiny Quest⍵ Ministries & Life Coaching
Helping people find their destiny and purpose
(Eph 4:11&12)

Dedication

I want to dedicate this book to my family whom I love with all my being.

Matthew 12:46-50
While Yeshua was still speaking to the crowds, His mother and brothers were standing outside, trying to speak to Him. Someone said to Him, "Look, Your mother and Your brothers are standing outside, trying to speak to You."

But to the one telling Him this, Yeshua responded, "Who is My mother? And who are My brothers?" Stretching out His hand toward His disciples, He said, "Here are My mother and My brothers. For whoever does the will of My Father in heaven, he is My brother and sister and mother."

TABLE OF CONTENTS

INTRODUCTION……………………………….6
HOW DID I GET HERE?…………………………8
WHO IS HERE?……………………………………24
WHY AM I HERE?………………………………..63
WHERE AM I GOING NEXT?………………….83
YOUR TURN………………………………………..88
WHO AM I?…………………………………………94
WHERE AM I GOING?…………………………106
AFTERWORD…………………………………..113

INTRODUCTION

Revelation 12:11 (TLV)

They overcame him by the blood of the Lamb and by the word of their testimony, and they did not love their lives even in the face of death.

    This book is my testimony entailing my life's journey thus far. My intention for releasing this writing is to impart revelatory knowledge in hopes that the reader recognizes the Love of GOD within its pages. Everything I have experienced has contributed to the person I am and will become. As a child, I used to hear the Elders say, "I don't know where I'd be if the Lord hadn't been on my side." That is truly a profound statement. Before we go any further let's take a little detour down the road to salvation. If you have not accepted Jesus as Lord and didn't know why you should, here's a brief explanation on the importance of doing so:

Romans 1:16
For I am not ashamed of the Good News, for it is the power of God for salvation to everyone who trusts—to the Jew first and also to the Greek.

Romans 2:9-11
There will be trouble and hardship for every human soul that does evil—to the Jew first and also to the Greek. [10] But there will be glory, honor,

and shalom to everyone who does good—to the Jew first and also to the Greek. [11] For there is no partiality with God.

Romans 10:12
For there is no distinction between Jew and Greek, for the same Lord is Lord of all—richly generous to all who call on Him.

Romans 10:10
For with the heart it is believed for righteousness, and with the mouth, it is confessed for salvation.

Now, acknowledge that you want to change and no longer desire to live in sin without Jesus. Ask Him to take complete control of your life (mind, body, and soul), use your own words. Begin to thank Him for loving you. Now is a good time to offer Him words of praise, worship, and adoration. It doesn't have to be fancy, GOD knows your heart, and He is proud of you for taking this step.

WELCOME TO THE FAMILY! HEAVEN IS REJOICING!

Lord, lead and guide your child to the place that you have lovingly prepared to receive them and train them up in Your ways so they may grow into the vessel you have predetermined them to be.

Let's begin.

HOW DID I GET HERE?

Proverbs 20:24

A man's steps are directed by ADONAI.

How then can anyone understand his own way?

I am currently a resident of Alamogordo New Mexico. A question I get all the time is 'What brought you to Alamogordo?' My answer is always GOD. After the curious looks I proceed with, "GOD told me to follow my husband to New Mexico, and I said but GOD I don't like him, and I don't even have a passport." Has anyone heard of Alamogordo? I hadn't. Since arriving I know it's the desert home to Holloman Air Force Base, White Sands National Monument, and a NASA Space Museum. Alamogordo means, "big cottonwood" in Spanish. It's associated with the Trinity Site, which is where the first atomic bomb was tested, and it's also the place where I was abused, abandoned, neglected, cheated on, called to, given Authority in, and where I am fulfilling my destiny.

In October of 2014, while living in Rockmart Georgia, I was observing GODS Holy Days, Rosh Hashanah and Yom Kippur. Rosh Hashanah, also known as The Festival of Trumpets is celebrated as GOD's New Year and the time to renew your bond with GOD. Yom Kippur is The Day of Atonement with GOD and others. It is observed with repentance, fasting, and prayer. I was seeking and searching for answers in my life. I was hurt, broken, and knew there had to be more to my life and relationship with GOD than what I was currently experiencing. Observing Rosh Hashanah, The Days of Awe, and Yom Kippur would surely give me the answers I was searching for. Growing up in Brooklyn I was exposed to the Jewish community. There was something about them I couldn't quite put my finger on. The way they carried themselves and the favor and influence they exuded. I remember wanting to be Jewish as a kid because they had so many celebrations.

So, as I was fasting for Yom Kippur, I saw my husband's face. It caused some strange emotions because I was really upset with him because our oldest son had run away to be with him in New Mexico. I assumed I was seeing my estranged husband's face because God was telling me to forgive him and to pray for him. I wanted to be obedient, so that's exactly what I did.

A few days later at work, I had a strong sense to call my oldest son and give him my phone number. Two days later I received a call from my son telling me that his dad was on his way back to New Mexico from New York and my son wanted me and his two younger siblings to accompany their dad to New Mexico to celebrate my oldest sons 17th birthday. I told my son that would never happen! I was going nowhere with his father, but I wished him a Happy Birthday, and I told him that I would send his siblings to spend his birthday with him. I told him that it was alright if he gave his dad my phone number so that we could coordinate our meeting place, so he could retrieve the children and take them to New Mexico. My estranged husband called me and shared that GOD had told him to come to Georgia to get his family because GOD wanted to reconcile his family. I immediately shouted 'Satan, THE LORD REBUKE YOU!' I am not going anywhere with you. We talked a short while, and I sent him my address so that he could map out his trip. I didn't get a wink of sleep. I kept seeing his face.

When I woke that morning I heard, "Leave everything and follow your husband." I didn't believe that was GOD, so I dismissed it. When I arrived at work that morning, I heard the same thing only louder, and then the Fear of The Lord came over me so strong I almost ran back to my car. At that moment I knew it was GOD and I was shaking as I entered my key and code to gain access to the building as I ignorantly said, "but GOD, I don't have a passport?" I went into my office and typed up my resignation letter. Once I sent it, I immediately felt the Joy of The Lord envelop me, and I couldn't stop laughing. I felt like I had lost a few pounds because I felt so weightless. I went to the Administrative Assistant's office and handed her my keys, told her I sent in my resignation and that I was quitting. I left and have never looked back.

I called my husband and told him what I did, and he couldn't believe it. At that moment he was traveling through Tennessee, so I went home to pack. GOD told me to leave everything! I was able to pack a suitcase for myself, take my laptop and our vital records. When the children came home to see their dad, they were ecstatic. I told them to pack a suitcase because we were only going for a week. I was still fighting what GOD had previously said. We drove to my brother's house and dropped off my apartment and car keys and left instructions for them to please clean out my apartment, give the car keys to my Bishop, and take whatever furniture and food they wanted.

    What GOD spoke to me while I was packing was that HE was sending me to a place that the Gifts HE invested in me would be used like never before. HE said out of my belly would flow rivers of living water. That made no sense to me because Alamogordo is a desert, doesn't GOD have a sense of humor? That's why HIS ways are not our ways, and HIS thoughts are not our thoughts because I couldn't make sense out of the message, I just knew I had to obey. It felt like life depended on my obedience and not just my life was tied into my obedience. All things work together for good to those who love GOD and are called according to HIS purpose means just that, ALL things.

We left Georgia on a Friday evening and arrived in Alamogordo, New Mexico, on a Sunday afternoon. It was beautiful! Immediately I fell in love with the landscape. I had never seen mountains so close before. Breathtaking! The clouds seem to be playing hide and seek with the mountains. The view from the wrap around porch of my husband's rental property bought tears to my eyes. I felt so much peace and love in the atmosphere. After taking in the view, I went to unpack. I opened the closet door and saw women's clothes; my mouth dropped open, and my stomach sank. My husband explained that his mistress didn't take her clothes when she left New Mexico. WHAT THE HELL! It's all I thought. No words came out of my mouth, and at that moment I knew The Holy Spirit had complete control of my faculties.

There was an argument going on between my soul and my spirit. Because I had fasted previously, my soul had no control. THANK GOD! My spirit was in complete control of my body and communication was only that of Heaven. That's the Omniscience of GOD in operation. GOD knows me and knows I struggled with an unpleasant habit of acting first. What was the purpose of HIM sending me to Alamogordo just to be arrested? In HIS Omniscience a burden was placed within me to fast and pray and seek HIS will long before I even knew about moving to New Mexico. I know you've heard it a thousand times before: nothing takes GOD by surprise. HE already knows the end from the beginning because HE operates outside of time. I can testify that if you keep your mind on JESUS, HE will keep you in perfect peace. I couldn't argue even if I wanted to because there was no offense in me. You see, when you are fully immersed in JESUS what goes on around you can't offend you because there is no offense in JESUS only in the flesh. I know what unclean spirits were controlling my ex. I also know that GOD loves him dearly and is the GOD of restoration and reconciliation. The assignment I received is spiritual, so the attack is spiritual. I know that what happens in the spirit manifests in the natural. So, this war is going on in the spirit and affecting my natural.

To fight back in the natural is useless in a spiritual battle. The blessing is that I didn't feel the gut punches; remember, GOD had me fasting. GLORY HALLELUJAH! Because I fasted, my flesh was subject to my spirit; and my spirit was fully aligned to GOD'S Heavenly channel or frequency. Therefore, HIS voice was dominant in my heart. The hurt, pain, and disappointment could not cloud my thought patterns; my soul was under subjection to CHRIST. That's what it means to take every thought captive under the obedience of JESUS CHRIST. This would have been a much different account that could have included bail money. TO GOD BE THE GLORY!

After staying at the house for two days, my husband's landlord showed up threatening to evict him. I was then introduced as the "wife." The landlord was very blunt and straightforward when she asked me, WHY was I here and married to him!? She shared that he moved into her rental property with another woman and hadn't been paying the rent. I told her I did not know what transpired before I arrived but that I was here to stay with my family. I so wanted to step outside of my body and look me in the eyes! I couldn't believe the words that were coming out of my mouth! The next day we moved to a hotel while my husband figured out our living arrangement. My son was staying with friends, so we didn't see him that much. After being at the hotel for three days, the children and I were moved into a trailer. I thought it was a nice place. I had never been in a trailer before, and it was not at all what I expected. It was a double wide, very roomy with 3 decent sized bedrooms and 2 nice sized bathrooms. Everything was modern, and there was even a front porch. After the second night in the new place, I realized that my loving, devoted husband and father of our children moved us into a drug spot! JESUS! His friend who owned the trailer sold drugs out of the trailer prior to us moving in.

When my husband relayed the need for a home for his wife and children the friend moved in with his girlfriend and allowed us to stay in the trailer. He just forgot to give all his customers his forwarding address! I still didn't argue, nor did I talk much English, my words were mostly my heavenly language.

It was Thanksgiving week. The weather had just begun to change, and we were making plans for our first time in years to celebrate Thanksgiving as a family. My husband had been seeing a therapist because he knew something was wrong with him. He was given a mental health diagnosis and prescribed a cocktail of really potent meds. It was rough, and he was having a hard time getting adjusted to the meds when he had a psychotic break and tried to kill me. He was hearing voices and thought I was saying and doing things that were not real. He pulled out a butcher knife and our eldest son put himself in the middle of us. I don't remember much of what was said, what I do remember is hearing *"when the enemy comes in like a flood, the Spirit of The Lord will lift up a standard against him. (Isa 59:19b)"*. It felt like my body was seizing, but it was not natural. I heard my heavenly language like never before. I also heard my husband repeatedly tell me to shut up. He even put his hand over my mouth, but I could not stop convulsing and speaking in tongues. He called me crazy and left the room, and I didn't see him again until the next morning.

That next morning was Thanksgiving Eve, and I didn't know what was in store for me. I remember asking GOD if my assignment was over?

Can I go to California now? I knew I was not going back to Georgia; I was so excited to be out of the spiritual oppression of the Bible Belt. I was ready to go west. My husband thought I stole his iPhone 6 and he lost it. He broke my laptop, and that was it! I thought *"I don't care what spiritual influence he's under; I'll pray for him later, right now I'm going to lay hands on him because I've had enough!"* Mind you; he's 6ft tall and 325lbs to my 5ft and 230! What was I thinking? When he broke my laptop, I heard the kids scream, and I came to my senses. I then went into the kid's bedroom and called the police. Our first Thanksgiving in New Mexico was spent in a battered women's shelter. They offered to give me and my children bus fare to get back to Georgia. I couldn't accept it; because even in all that we just endured, I knew GOD had a purpose for my children and me right here in Alamogordo. So that is how I came to be a resident of Alamogordo, New Mexico and where I began to operate in the spirit realm as never before.

WHO IS HERE?

2 Cor 5:17

Therefore, if any person is [ingrafted] in Christ (the Messiah) he is a new creation (a new creature altogether); the old [previous moral and spiritual condition] has passed away. Behold, the fresh and new has come!

There is a lie circulating that Believers are sinners saved by grace. That could not be further from the truth. Romans 5:8, the scripture used to back up this error, says:

> **But God commendeth his love toward us, in that, while we were yet sinners, Christ died for us.**

In this verse, the word 'sinners' is the Greek word hamartólos which is an adjective. The root word in

Greek is ἁμαρτωλός, and it is a verb which describes an action or condition. The action or condition it is describing is:

1. be without;
2. to miss the mark (not share in the prize)
3. error or be mistaken
4. wander from uprightness or honor by doing wrong
5. wander from God's law.

Romans 5:8 does not name us sinners. God clearly shows and proves HIS love for us because while we were without him or we missed the mark, or we were mistaken, or we wandered from his uprightness, Jesus still died for us. Numbers 23:8 asks a question:

> ***How can I curse those whom God has not cursed? How can I***

denounce those whom the LORD has not denounced?

This includes us as well. I must catch myself and repent of speaking curses over myself, others, the government, etc. Self-deprecation is a lie from the pit of hell. It is false humility and goes against GOD's Word. Deprecation is to pray against someone or something. The Latin root is 'precari' which means to pray. When you add the 'de' to a word you reverse or undo the original meaning. We are not to pray against anyone, anything, and especially not our selves.

I was born in Kings County Hospital located in Brooklyn, New York, on December 28, 1972. December is the 12th month of the Gregorian Calendar. The number 12 signifies GOD's Power and Authority as well as His perfect Governmental

Rule, hence the 12 Tribes of Israel and the 12 Gates of Heaven. In Hebrew Gematria (one of several methods of assigning a numerical value to a Hebrew name, word or phrase based on its letters), *koakh* means "power" and/or "energy" and corresponds to the number 28.

Mazzaroth is found in Job 38:31-33(ESV), and it means constellations.

> ***Can you bind the chains of the Pleiades or loose the cords of Orion?***
>
> ***Can you lead forth the Mazzaroth[b] in their season, or can you guide the Bear with its children? Do you know the ordinances of the heavens? Can you establish their rule on the earth?***

According to the Mazzaroth, I was born under the constellation of Capricornus. Capricornus is a figure of a creature that is half goat and half fish. Leviticus says that a goat was used to atone for sins. Matthew describes the fish as a symbol of restoration. I am essentially doing what I was created to do, teach people how to understand their purpose so they can choose Jesus' perfect gift of eternal life.

You and I are the Temple of the Holy Spirit. He chooses to dwell within us and lead us in His Truth. When I said "YES!" in 2004, I had no clue that I was lining my will up to His plan. Chronology in the Talmud (collection of Jewish law and tradition) is key. Capricornus is one of the last three months (winter) when the sun travels over the desert. According to Jewish tradition,-it is believed the sun takes this path, so the grain doesn't dry up and wither. I live in the desert! GOD HAS A SENSE OF HUMOR! If Satan had his way, I would not have made it this far. He has been trying to kill me since I was a child. Our destinies are written in the stars. Astrology is a perversion of a Godly resource. I don't need a horoscope to dictate my day, because GOD already prophesied my existence and wrote it in the heavens for all to see, including me. Don't waste your time on a third party, go straight to the Source. A pet peeve of mine is if my child's friends ask my permission for my child to do something. I don't have a relationship with you, and you don't know me like that, my child does or should. I'm sure GOD feels the same way, ask Him. Our enemy perverts' things because we believe he has more authority than he does based on the events in the Garden of Eden. The rest of the story is found in 1 John 3:8 (TLV)

> ***The one who practices sin is of the devil, for the devil has been sinning from the beginning. <u>Ben-Elohim (SON of GOD) appeared for this purpose—to destroy the works of the devil.</u>*** (emphasis mine)

Jesus' life, death, and resurrection destroyed ALL the works of the enemy. Because HIS BLOOD was and will always be the perfect atonement for ALL sin committed, WE WIN, WE ARE THE CHAMPIONS OF THE WORLD!

I am the first of three children born to my parents. I come from a pretty big family on both sides. My father has six other siblings, and my mother has 17. Growing up in New York was fun because I was surrounded by both sides of my family. Most weekends were a celebration of some sort. I was blessed to be raised around my paternal and maternal grandparents.

My paternal grandparents didn't live together. Grandpa Al had a window treatment store in Brooklyn that my dad worked at sometimes. My grandpa was loud and funny. He had to be loud because there was a machine in the back of the shop that cut the shades to the right size of the window and it was loud. My grandpa was at least 6 ft tall, muscular and had dark wavy hair. He had beautiful cocoa skin and a nice singing voice. He played the piano too. Sometimes instead of me being at the shop with my grandpa, dad, and uncle, I would be at my grandpa's apartment around the corner. During lunch or after work grandpa would sit me on his lap at the piano and play a tune. Grandpa was an Army Veteran too. He was of Cuban and West Indian descent but couldn't speak a lick of Spanish. He used to say some German phrases he picked up during his time serving overseas in Germany.

My maternal grandmother was a live-in home health nurse. Grandma Maxine taught me how to take care of people. She was a great caretaker who treated her patients like they were family. Every time I would visit, the house always smelled like bleach. If you sat down too long, you'd get bleached too. Grandma was a superb cook as well. She used to make my favorites: pot roast, fresh green beans and mashed potatoes with gravy. For dessert, she would make banana pudding with meringue. I tasted the love she has for me in every bite. To this day I associate beautiful music and food with the love I felt from my paternal grandparents. They gave me what they had and taught me so much more than they, or I, could ever realize at the time.

My maternal grandparents lived in a Brooklyn brownstone. The home is still in the family. Grandpa Mac worked outside of the home, and Grandma Eva worked in the home. Grandpa Mac was short and bowlegged. He walked like he just hopped off a horse. My fondest memories with him were listening to baseball games on the radio and eating his favorite snacks: ginger snaps, cheddar cheese, and boiled peanuts. Grandpa would occasionally come home with a surprise, sugar cane. Our cherished game was "gimme a kiss gurl!" Grandpa Mac would tickle my cheek, chin, neck area with his unshaven beard while giving me kisses. Everyone knew that when Grandpa came home, you had to vacate his favorite wing-backed chair.

Grandma Eva was the neighborhood Mother. All you had to do was come knocking, and she would whip you up something homemade. Grandma used to have a garden in the back yard, and I loved snapping peas with her, one for the pot and one for me. Before I even knew what the Presence of GOD was, I felt it in Grandma Eva's kitchen. The radio would be on and she and her sister, Thelma (everyone called her "Sister"), would be in the kitchen humming, singing, praying, praising GOD and listening to sermons. I was one of 25 grandkids and never felt neglected. I remember one time when I slept at my grandparents' house after watching the news my

Grandma would get on her knees and begin to pray. I was down there with her, but I was finished long before she was. She was down there so long I thought she fell asleep. The next day I asked her why she fell asleep on her knees. She said she didn't fall asleep she was praying. I remarked that she was down there so long. She said she had a lot to pray for and she surely did; she had 18 children, need I elaborate?

Growing up I remember people remarking on how smart, funny, and quick I was. We used to have relay races and beat all the other girls and boys. I loved to read, and I felt so much love and joy being around my extended family. The older I became, the more I was exposed to instances that showed a different side of my fun-loving, happy family. There was so much dysfunction that I don't know where exactly to begin. The worst part of it all is that for some reason the Baby Boomer generation in my family doesn't talk about problems. They act as if problems don't exist. I guess that is their coping mechanism. I had so many questions, but there was no one to give me answers, so I decided to stop asking and not deal with anyone except my imaginary friend, JESUS. I would talk to JESUS all the time, and HE would always play with me, and I would always feel at peace.

    The older I became, the more I struggled with identity and the more depressed I became because I had no one who could answer my questions. I was a good student in school because learning was easy. I read tons of books because they helped me imagine life outside of my current circumstances. I lived in an abusive household; and

I didn't sleep well, because I was afraid I would wake up to find that my father had killed my mother.

I was a very nervous and subservient child. I bit my nails until they bled. I always wanted to please my parents so there would be no fighting or arguing. I even stuttered because I was always afraid of saying something that would make others upset or uncomfortable. Carrying this into my teenage years was the perfect ingredient to foster low self-esteem. I went from attempting to please my parents to pleasing everyone. All the while I was miserable inside and often had suicidal thoughts and ideas.

I loved to read to take me out of my reality. I read any and everything from the Holy Bible to dime store novels and everything in between. I loved words and their meaning so much I would read the dictionary and encyclopedias insatiably because I just wanted to know everything about the world around me because it had to be better than the world in which I was imprisoned.

In Junior High School I met who I thought was the love of my life. I was an eighth grader, a senior, and I had all the answers in life. I gave away my virginity and shortly after became a 15-year-old mother. I hid my pregnancy from my parents. I remember my first birds and the bees talk with my mother. She said to me in passing, "if you get pregnant before you graduate High School, I'm gonna whoop your @$&!" What she didn't know was that I was three months pregnant by the time she got around to warn me. I finally told my parents I was pregnant, and they took me to an abortion clinic. During my examination, the nurse asked me what was wrong. I told her my parents were making me kill my baby. The nurse said I had the right to have my baby. She called my mother in the room and explained that no one could force me to terminate the pregnancy. My mother was furious! She yelled "WHO'S GONNA TAKE CARE OF THIS DAMNED BABY! I CAN'T AFFORD ANOTHER MOUTH TO FEED. SHE BARELY MADE IT INTO 9TH GRADE, AND THE BABY'S DADDY IS IN 10TH!"

  I hadn't thought about how I would take care of this child. The only thing I knew was that I loved her, and I needed her just as much as she would need me. I didn't know the sex at that time, I just wanted a daughter, so I could give her all the love and attention I craved. My parents didn't speak to me for weeks. I decided it was best if I left so I wouldn't be a burden. So, I ran away to a teen shelter in Lower Manhattan. Two days later I was called into the office at the shelter, and there was my mother sitting there. I was shocked that she came for me. I thought she didn't love me anymore because I had royally messed up.

    My daughters' father treated me like I had an infectious disease. I went to tell his mother she was expecting a grandchild and she told me it might not be her sons and even if it was, he didn't have to do anything he didn't want to do regarding fatherhood. I was crushed! I tried everything my young adolescent mind could fathom to get his attention and regain his love, but of course, nothing worked. Shortly after our first child's birth, he moved down south to finish high school. True to his mother's declaration, he chose not to be a part of how our child was raised. That was the first time I tried to end what I deemed as a useless existence. I swallowed a whole bottle of aspirin and threw up for hours.

My parents didn't make it easy on me either. They loved that baby but made sure I understood she was my responsibility. I didn't know that babies can suffer from trauma. I had an emotionally draining pregnancy and cried a lot. My baby cried a lot if she wasn't being held. Everywhere I went she went because she was my responsibility. I am grateful for my parent's stance on that. My oldest daughter is very beautiful and intelligent. At three years old I thought she was a genius. Her favorite book was "Hop on Pop" by Dr. Seuss. One day she brought the book to me to show me she could read it, and she did front to back. I ran in the living room to tell my dad. His eyes got wide then he said, "wait, let me see something." He turned to the last page and had her read. She began to recite from memory page 1. This three-year-old memorized her favorite book. I was proud of her, but she wouldn't be in the Guinness Book of World Records for the youngest reader.

Two years later I had my second child by a different young man. Here I am a 17-year-old unemployed mother of two beautiful children. One day I heard my Uncle talking to my parents about me, and he said something like, "Well she's just another statistic now. She has two children by two different men and hasn't even graduated high school. The best we can hope for is that she gets a job and doesn't get on welfare, and hopefully doesn't have any more children."

Almost 30 years later those words try to infiltrate my subconscious and settle into my spirit to attempt to choke the life of The Word of GOD right out of me. Before I was formed in my mother's womb, GOD had a plan for me. Jeremiah 29:11 declares:

> **For I know the thoughts that I think toward you, says the LORD, thoughts of peace and not of evil, to give you a future and a hope.**

The word *thoughts* that occurs twice in this New King James Version is the Hebrew word **machashabah** which means intentions or plans. So even though it looked like I royally screwed up my life by birthing two beautiful daughters before I was

18, GOD had already devised peace instead of evil in the future HE expected for me.

My babies were my world. I took care of them the best way I knew how. I gave them everything I felt I didn't have. People say New York City is expensive, but there are things you can do for little to nothing or even for free. The Bronx Zoo has free admission on Wednesdays. Different museums have free admission days as well. There are different parks and free concerts going on throughout the city. We lived in Coney Island with the beach as our backyard. In the 1990's I felt safe raising my babies in the City. The problem was I only had a GED and jobs required at least an Associate's Degree to make any real money.

I left New York City in the summer of 1995 to visit my best friend who had moved to Pennsylvania. I was tired of living with my parents, and the rents in New York City were ridiculously high. My "bff" had assured me that Pennsylvania was more affordable and a safer place to raise her niece and goddaughter. (My first child's father was her brother in law and my second child was her goddaughter.) We had known each other since elementary school because I would sometimes visit her church with my neighbors who also attended.

I was in Pennsylvania for about a week when I was arrested for assault. My children were outside on the lawn playing when a drunk woman in her thirties swerved into the parking lot at 11:00 a.m. and almost hit my youngest daughter. I sat on the balcony in shock feeling helpless because my child was almost run over. I went downstairs to knock on the neighbors' door and ask what was wrong with her, didn't she see my kid in the grass? I knocked on the door and asked the lady if she saw my daughter and; if so, why wasn't she more careful? She said I needed to keep my n!$%a kids out of her way! The next thing I knew, my friend and the lady's son were dragging me off her. I had punched her in the face knocking her to the ground and attempted to stomp her! All I saw was red, and I felt the rage! The police knocked on my friend's door 20 minutes later, and I was arrested. My bail was $1,000. I was told that when my bail was posted, I needed to go back to NYC with that mess because my behavior wasn't welcomed in Allentown, PA.

I did leave Allentown… every two weeks to visit my family in New York City and slowly transport my children and my clothing to Pennsylvania. I had no more run-ins with the neighbor. I decided this was my chance at a new life. I got involved with my "bff's" brother, and we eventually became engaged. I felt it could work because he was older and was a hard worker and he aspired to go into the ministry. The problem was I didn't love him. When an Alpha male came sniffing around, I cheated on my fiancé. My excuse for disrespecting him was that he wasn't assertive enough for me. The truth was that I had no idea who I was, so I didn't understand how I deserved to be treated. My fiancé was accommodating, kind, gentle, a listener, and a lover of GOD. The person I cheated with and ultimately married was a thug.

Just how I liked my men because I was a ride or die chick. How ignorant was I?

My new "Man" and I moved back to New York City where we both had family ties. After I gave birth to our first son in 1997, we knew we didn't want to raise him and his siblings in the city. It wasn't the safe place we had been raised in. It was rapidly changing for the worse. We eventually moved to Emmaus, Pennsylvania. Yes, I had an Emmaus road experience! While living in Emmaus, I began working for Bank of America and GOD introduced me to the person He would use to get me into the local church that He had personally picked out for my family and I. The ministry was founded by a woman, and one of her daughters was the Presiding Pastor. This was important to me because I didn't have a good relationship with my mother while growing up, and GOD used this ministry to heal that part of my soul. HE brought me to that Local Body to show me how to be His Princess.

During that time, I didn't have a vehicle, but my coworker always offered to bring my three children and me. I loved attending because the choir was off the chain! I was always entertained, and the Pastor looked like Diana Ross, she was beautiful with big hair and could sing like Mahalia Jackson! After a while, the nostalgia wore off because I didn't go to church to get closer to GOD. I went to be entertained. I was still living in sin with my baby daddy, still smoking cigarettes and still drinking. The church was cramping my lifestyle and making me uncomfortable, so it was either give it up or give up my sin. I chose to sin.

One day I was at the mall and saw the Pastor. I tried to duck into a store quick so that she wouldn't see me, but I wasn't fast enough. She called my name, and I pointed to myself and asked, "who me?' DUH! I remember asking her how she remembered my name. She said GOD told her. I wanted to call her a liar because that made no sense, but inside I knew she was telling the truth. I remember her inviting me to come back anytime, and I said I wouldn't lie and make any promises. She said she respected that and went on her way.

  I don't remember how long after our encounter it took me to return to church, but I did return. This time I didn't just attend service, I was at Sunday school as well as learning the Word. This is a Pentecostal Church that believes Sunday is the Lords day so don't make plans that don't include

Him. I would arrive at 8:15 a.m. and not get out of service until around 3:00 p.m. (if the service wasn't that "high"), or 5:00 p.m. (if The Holy Ghost was setting people free). My children and I attended Tuesday evening Pastoral teaching and Wednesday night prayer, along with Sunday service and any other special services. To those on the outside looking in it was a bit extreme, but I needed to tear down the walls I had built up during my lifetime by immersing myself in GOD. This resulted in HIS foundation being established in me during the time we attended this church. People often remark at how I am anointed to pray. I received an impartation for prayer and the prophetic through that ministry. That is a powerful prophetic praying ministry! All the years I served at the ministry I was exposed to The Manifest Power of GOD. I saw demonic and angelic activity. I saw demons cast out and I felt the Glory of GOD arrest us. I saw children as young as four years old receive the Baptism of the Holy Spirit, evidenced by speaking their Heavenly language. I saw the spirit realm up close and personal and was taught how to hear His voice. Just like the men on the Emmaus road, I didn't realize the magnitude or importance of what was happening as I was being taught to walk out my soul salvation. Thank GOD He wasn't through with me, by far.

I was 25 when I left New York City. Twenty–five signifies grace upon grace. I spent 10-years in Pennsylvania. The biblical meaning of 10 is completed a course of time or completeness in divine order. My next destination would be Georgia for 6 years. The number 6 symbolizes man's/woman's weakness. 2 Corinthians 12:9-10 (TLV):

> ***But He said to me, "My grace is sufficient for you, for power is made perfect in weakness." Therefore, I will boast all the more gladly in my weaknesses, so that the power of Messiah may dwell in me. *[10]* For Messiah's sake, then, I delight in weaknesses, in insults, in distresses, in persecutions, in calamities. For when I am weak, then I am strong.***

My parents and siblings no longer lived in New York City, they were now Georgians. My parents bought a house in Hiram, GA. My sister, her children, and my oldest daughter lived in Lawrenceville. While my brother and his family lived in Dallas, GA. I decided to reside closer to my parents. This move took place in June of 2008. I had so many plans for my life when I arrived. I had left my husband because I didn't want to raise my children in an abusive household and continue the cycle. I took my 401k payout from the Pennsylvania Department of Labor and Industry with the intention of purchasing a home for my babies and me. The problem was, the job market was freezing up due to the economy. I couldn't even get a job at any of the Dollar stores.

GOD blessed me with unemployment, so I didn't have to stress work, so I decided to go to school to learn a different skill set. My three youngest children and I were living in one bedroom in my parents' two-bedroom townhome. It was great at first, but the honeymoon didn't last long.

Even though I purchased the food and had dinner ready when they came home from work, I was still made to feel like I was a burden. My children were too loud, or I wasn't allowed to use the computer to do my school work, it was always something. After a few months, I started getting angry with this situation. How could my parents mistreat me? I know how to be in a home without you ever knowing I was there, but even that was a problem because my parents thought I was keeping the kids locked up in the room all day so I could sleep. However, that was not the case. I just didn't want to hear anyone complaining. I eventually moved and stayed with each sibling until that too became uncomfortable for my three children and I. So, we moved to an Econo Lodge near my parent's subdivision.

I know it sounds horrible, and it was, but there is a purpose in everything. You've heard the saying "hurt people hurt people?" That is the truest statement outside of scripture. I didn't realize the depth of my parents' pain. They each have their own demons to contend with. As I previously stated, they don't talk about the elephant in the room. That gives them a false sense of security because they think that not talking about something makes it less real. NOT! Therefore, they are eternally tormented by the past. Leaving their home was not a bad thing. I didn't live the same way as my parents or siblings. I was living for Jesus. Our spirits didn't walk in agreement at all; and since I lived in their homes. I had to go -- but not far. GOD wanted me to forgive the past.

My conversation with GOD went like this: "You bring me to a place where I am supposed to be safe because family surrounds me and I am homeless with three small children? How do you expect me to forgive?" GOD told me He bought me back to the beginning to heal because I couldn't go forward until I dealt with the past. My childhood was filled with trauma due to addiction. I said I forgave my parents, but that theory was never tested because they lived in Georgia and I lived in Pennsylvania. Now I had the opportunity to test my belief, and it didn't start well. I can remember one day telling my father "the only reason you're still breathing is that I love Jesus and He doesn't want me to kill you!" After that I promised myself, I would never speak to him ever again. Thank GOD I didn't keep that promise.

I was led to a church that began to help me heal. One day I was waiting for my youngest daughter to be released from dance rehearsal and the Pastor stopped to talk to me. He said "Daughter..." I didn't hear much after that because the tears began to flow. See, he didn't know what I was going through, but GOD did, and He was speaking to my brokenness through the Pastor. The Pastor was confused and asked me why I was crying, and I couldn't talk. Sometime later I shared the reason for my unusual behavior, and he understood. That was the beginning of my healing process. That Pastor was used to break up fallow ground in me, so I could begin to receive the Love, Word, and Will of GOD. I was instructed by GOD not to join that ministry. I was only there for a season, but I was not to stay. At first, I listened, but as time progressed, I felt weird not officially joining. During one service the doors of the church were opened, and the hand of fellowship was extended. I ran up there to accept! Shortly after, all hell broke loose, and I left the ministry. Obedience is better than sacrifice.

That was it for me! Every time I took two steps forward, I was knocked back 10, and I decided I was not going to church again. I could watch church on television and still get blessed. While volunteering at my children's school, one of the teachers invited me to an Anniversary Church Service. I pretended to listen, all the while planning on NOT attending, or so I thought. That Sunday evening, I found myself pulling up to the church. I don't remember the message. What I do remember is getting up off the floor. I had not danced before the Lord in years. I was told later on that there was no music playing, I just began to dance around the church when the Bishop spoke that GOD was restoring my joy. My children and I began attending this ministry and received invaluable instruction on how to study the Word and walk in our calling.

Before GOD moved me to New Mexico, I worked hard to forgive my parents. It's easy to pass judgment in hindsight. People can't give what they don't have. Brokenness that is not yielded to GOD produces after its kind, more brokenness. There are millions of lovers of GOD who are housing decades of trauma. GOD showed me who my parents are to Him and that helped me forgive them and heal. I always pray that they accept the Love of GOD and walk in the freedom Jesus paid dearly for. I have come to terms with the knowledge that a prophet is not welcomed in his hometown. It doesn't have to be me that disciples them.

In Pennsylvania, GOD showed me my identity: a Princess. I embraced my value as a woman and celebrated my femininity and was shown how to be a lady. In Georgia, I was freed to be a daughter who could receive from her Abba Father because I trusted Him. The Love of GOD is so apparent throughout His Word. I can honestly say living in Georgia was the worst time of my life naturally but the best time developmentally. The Bishop of the ministry my children and I attended is a Bible Scholar and taught us everything he knows. He is a graduate of Rhema Bible College and operates in a strong healing anointing. This ministry teaches how not only to read and study the Word of GOD, but it stresses the importance of the Word being active and apparent in the lives of ALL believers regardless of age. I was a part of this Body for four years and was licensed as an Evangelist under this ministry. The number four symbolizes God setting all things in order. That is why the person who arrived in New Mexico in October of 2014 was ready to walk in the path GOD had predetermined for me.

WHY AM I HERE?

Jeremiah 29:11 (KJV)
For I know the thoughts that I think toward you, saith the LORD, thoughts of peace, and not of evil, to give you an expected end.

I love the origin and meaning of words, so I did an exhaustive study on the above scripture, and GOD spoke to me through it. This is what HE said to me:

> *I know everything there is and ever will be known about you. My plan calls for your participation, so I decreed your existence because I AM YEHOVAH and my purpose is for you to exist in complete health and wealth; to destroy the effects of chaos and to bestow hope to future generations.*

My name is Crystal. Revelation 4:6 describes Crystal as clear/transparent, and Revelation 21:11 describes Crystal as a precious jewel shining with The Glory of GOD. Crystal is a form of Flint Rock. Flint is sedimentary, foundational. Flint is also said to be easy to shape, and because of this, it is shaved into a spear with pointy edges. Flint aids in frequency/energy shift, a conduit and used to start a flame.

GOD bought me to New Mexico to establish HIS Truth. Everyone has their version of the truth based on information and experience received. What someone believes is what they hold as truth. What I've learned is that our truths are sometimes fluid. What we believe today may not be the same in the near or distant future. That's not the case with

GOD. HIS Truth is eternal and never has nor will ever change.

One day when I was crying out to HIM. I was in the spirit and before a throne. I saw JESUS on the right hand of the FATHER. There were lots of people around. I fell to my knees like the Prophet Isaiah and began to weep. I felt so unworthy and unclean. At that moment Jesus came over to me and put a white robe or cloak on my shoulders and a crown and told me to rise. I kept pleading with him to leave me there because I was unworthy and didn't deserve to be in his presence. HE told me that I was called to this place of authority and he was going to use me for his glory. I cried tears of joy and relief. Over the next several months Jesus began teaching me about the spirit realm. He connected me to several groups via social media, and that is when I was introduced to Robert Henderson's teaching on the Courts of Heaven and Mike Parsons mentorship ministry, Engaging GOD Programme (he is from England, and this is how they spell "program"). You can connect with each of these ministries (if GOD leads you to). The way Mike teaches is perfect for my learning style. I am a multisensory learner, and he uses lots of aids. Everything is hands on so you learn by doing.

As a child, I was familiar with the spirit realm. During my teenage and young adult years, I ran full speed away from GOD to do my own thing and ran right into Him. I was reacquainted with the supernatural when I lived in Pennsylvania. Georgia took me through my wilderness, and now that I am in New Mexico I am told to inhabit my promised land. This mandate is not just about geography; it's about the supernatural too.

I didn't think my prayers were being answered in New Mexico. I wasn't sure exactly what was going on, but I needed a new way to pray. I stumbled upon this Facebook group that was teaching on prayer from a different perspective, and that's how I came across Apostle Robert Henderson's book, "Operating in the Courts of Heaven." I was fascinated and had so many questions, so I began to google anything on the Courts of Heaven, and that's where I encountered Mike Parsons. Mike has a video on YouTube in which he explains how he fasted for 40 days, as directed by GOD, and was changed by his heavenly encounters. I subscribed to his mentoring program, and the rest is history.

One day I was at work typing on the computer, and I kept hearing a song playing in my head. I googled the words, and it was Oceans by Hillsong (CCLI Song #6428767). I immediately pulled it up on my phone and put in my earbuds. There is a part in the song where it says:

> ***Spirit lead me where my***
>
> ***trust is without borders***
>
> ***Let me walk upon the waters***
>
> ***Wherever You would call me***
>
> ***Take me deeper than my***
>
> ***feet could ever wander***
>
> ***And my faith will be made stronger***
>
> ***In the presence of my Savior***

As I am sitting at my desk typing, I see a hand in front of me beckoning me. I immediately hear the scripture when Peter says Lord if that is you command me to come, I knew it was Jesus. I reached out for him, and we began to dance on the water. Tears flowed down my eyes uncontrollably! I was sitting in a cubicle in a very high traffic area. Usually, people walk by and speak to me all day, not then. It was like I was all alone with Jesus on the water.

When I first began to engage Heaven a few years ago, all my experiences were with Jesus, and when I was with Him, I was a little child. This made me curious, so I asked why? Jesus told me it was because that is when I innocently believed in Him before all the trauma in my life began. One day a friend was praying with me and remarked, Crystal, what is your problem with GOD? I was shocked and offended! What is she talking about? She said do you see GOD's face? I said no, you couldn't see

GOD and live. She said not your flesh; we're in the spirit right now. I began to well up, and the waterfall began.

"GOD HOW COULD YOU LET MY HUSBAND HURT ME! YOU BROUGHT ME ALL THE WAY HERE FOR ME TO BE ABUSED! I DON'T KNOW ANYONE, I AM ALL ALONE!"

I heard "I love you" in a whisper at first and then progressively louder. Then I saw the face of GOD for the first time since I could remember, and I saw all the LOVE and care He has for me. It was very intense. He called me His daughter, and when He said my name, I could feel my whole being beginning to vibrate, and I felt my purpose. That is when I understood who I am and why I am here.

I have been told I was beautiful, I have a beautiful smile, etc., and I took no stock in what was said. I didn't trust the source, so I always thought there was an ulterior motive behind the compliments. Our first realization of who we are comes from our parents. That is why GOD formed the family first, as a reflection of HIS relational desires for us. Our parents tell us who we are when we don't even understand the words they are saying, just like the Word of GOD; and we eventually begin to act according to what is being said or proclaimed. Growing up, I don't remember words of encouragement from my parents, I remember angry words. I'm not saying I wasn't told nice things; I don't remember them or the feelings associated with them.

My relationship with GOD has been developing my entire lifetime. Everything that has taken place in my life has been used at different times. For instance, I love to bless people with my home cooking because growing up I felt the love in both grandmothers' dishes. My father is brilliant and knows information about various subjects. He used to win family jeopardy all the time, so I love to learn mostly because I want to win!

I used to say, "I will never be like my parents!" In some ways, I became exactly what I feared. When I became angry, I could make the Queens Guard cry, and you know they are expressionless. One day I heard a message I had heard preached countless times before out of James 3:8-14 Tree of Life Version (TLV) about the unruliest member of our bodies, the tongue.

> *But no human being can tame the tongue. It is a restless evil, full of deadly poison. With it, we bless our ADONAI and Father, and with it, we curse people, who are made in the image of God. From the same mouth comes blessing and cursing. My brothers and sisters, these things should not be. A spring doesn't pour out fresh and bitter water from the same opening, does it? My brothers and sisters, can a fig tree produce olives, or a vine produce figs? Neither can salt water produce fresh water.*

After my encounters with GOD, there is no way I could continue with a reckless mouth. I had so much anger built up every time I was rubbed the wrong way, instead of me pronouncing blessings I was cussing up a storm. Saved, sanctified, Holy Ghost filled and on fire for GOD, but displaying ungodly character. Yes, I have been delivered, believe in fasting and prayer and praying in my heavenly language for at least an hour a day. So why was I still struggling with cussing? Mike Parsons has a series titled Transformation, it helped answer my questions and lead me to freedom. GOD took me to Hebrews 12:1-2

> **Therefore, since we have such a great cloud of witnesses surrounding us, let us also get rid of every weight and entangling sin. Let us run with endurance the race set before us, focusing on Yeshua, the**

initiator, and perfecter of faith. For the joy set before Him, He endured the cross, disregarding its shame; and He has taken His seat at the right hand of the throne of God.

I am the sum of my total parts. DNA has two strands which represent the union of man and woman. My blood carries the record of my ancestors: their hair, hands, eyes, mannerisms, even sins. Hebrews 12 illustrates to me that even though they missed the mark, there was a point in their lives when they accepted the perfect sacrifice because they are in heaven rooting for me. GOD doesn't want me stuck on how I keep getting it wrong. Instead, I am admonished to focus on the examples of getting it right. How do you do that? Glad you asked, repentance. You've probably been taught that repentance is telling GOD you're sorry. This is not exactly the route of long-term success. The best way to explain is to provide an example.

EXAMPLE:

> I was embarrassed that my internalized stress and anger resulted in a very foul mouth. I found curse words coming from my thoughts onto my tongue. I hoped my children wouldn't tell anyone. I felt guilty, and I had thoughts like, "You're not saved," "What will people think of you," and "You might as well go all in since all sin is the same." I cried out and confessed to GOD my struggles and that I didn't know what to do. As I was praying in tongues, I

saw my paternal grandmother in my memory going off on someone. She was giving someone a verbal stomping. Then I heard God say, "Familiar spirit." That's when GOD showed me what to do. HE had me submit my imagination to HIM. I saw myself in the spirit before The Lord. I saw the Great Cloud of Witnesses; the Just Men made perfect, the Seven Spirits of GOD and other inhabitants of Heaven. I was prompted to ask them to testify on behalf of my DNA. I could sense that there was great movement and joyful anticipation.

I called for the accusations that manifested in the language coming out of me. As each accusation was presented, I responded with a confession that I am guilty. Everything that was presented wasn't necessarily done by me, but because of a generational curse in my family, I still carried the record of the sin. I asked GOD to forgive me and my family, past, present, and future, for participating in the sin that so easily beset me and kept me at arm's length from receiving HIS Love. I then repented for my entire bloodline, and then I asked for the Blood of Jesus to testify on our behalf. Because the

Blood of Jesus is the only perfect sacrifice, the verdict presented by GOD the Father was "Not Guilty!" I asked for the proceedings to be recorded in my Book of Life, which is located in heaven; and for Angelic assistance to enforce the written order. Psalm 91:11 states the Angels watch over us to guard us in all our ways. Why not use every aid at our disposal.

I thanked GOD for loving me so much to set me free indeed! In the days ahead I was allowed to walk out the verdict, but instead of cussing, I began to speak the Word of GOD and come into agreement with His promises. These days I don't get tested as much.

I had the pleasure of leading an intercessory prayer group at Church. This was the opportunity GOD provided because He is raising spirit filled, spirit led intercessors for such a time as this. Everything I was being taught about the spirit realm I shared with this group. GOD told me from the beginning not to focus on the number of participants. Instead, I was to focus on the comprehension and application of the attendants. It was more important to make sure five people learned how to engage Him than for 50 to spectate. I love these people. When I first began to share my experiences, I could see the look on their faces. It was priceless. They could feel the power of GOD in what I was relaying, but they had no point of reference. Instead of not showing up they prayed to GOD and asked for clarification and confirmation that this was indeed Him. I was nervous and felt unqualified, but their hunger and willingness was the motivation I needed to press on. GOD never failed us and every meeting He met every one of us where we were.

One day I was in the shower, and I heard the sound of a trumpet heralding. It reminded me of a King Arthur movie I saw years ago. I was told to kneel when I did; I sensed a sword tapping my shoulders and I heard "You are named Repairer of The Breach." I humbly accepted and quickly finished in the shower so I could look up the meaning. I found it in Isaiah 58:12 (TLV)

> ***Some of you will rebuild the ancient ruins, will raise up the age-old***

foundations, will be called Repairer of the Breach, Restorer of Streets for Dwelling.

I am on this earth and particularly in Alamogordo, New Mexico to raise the standard of His foundations and restore His Truths. I don't always know who I will meet. I told GOD I am available for His service. It's not a walk in the park, and sometimes it gets lonely, but it's always worth it.

WHERE AM I GOING NEXT?

Isaiah 6:8 (NIV)

Then I heard the voice of the Lord saying, "Whom shall I send? And who will go for us?" And I said, "Here am I. Send me!"

I arrived in Alamogordo as a wife, but my marriage was dissolved by divorce decree on August 25, 2016, after being married for 10 years. However, before being married to my husband, we were living together outside of marriage for 10 years. We lived in sin for 10 years, during which time we had two children. Our third child arrived after we were married. We were committing fornication and still going to church. I was so convicted that I convinced myself it was better to marry than burn in Hell, even though GOD told me not to marry him. After all, what did GOD know? I figured that I could fast enough and pray enough to sanctify my husband, right?

Recently I became convicted of my disobedience. I began to cry out and repent for not listening to GOD about marrying when HE told me not to. I also cried for divorcing when I know divorce isn't GOD's will, because we are not to "put asunder" what HE has joined together (Matthew 19:6). That's when GOD set me free from guilt and remorse by telling me HE never joined us together. I married out of HIS will.

Now I've learned to listen to GOD and obey HIM. As I obey HIM, HE can trust me to do HIS will in HIS way.

GOD has shown me that HE has given me an international calling and ministry. In August of

2018, HE told me to begin a ministry and register it as a "for profit" company because The Kingdom of Heaven uses resources for advancement. It profits us much spiritually and naturally so why proclaim that it is not for profit when The Kingdom purpose is to multiply and produce after its kind? I will be traveling to many different nations. Growing up in Brooklyn, New York, has prepared me for travel. New York is a melting pot. You can go to different countries just by walking from neighborhood to neighborhood. There's Little Italy, Chinatown, Little Havana, etc. I was afforded the privilege of experiencing many different cultures growing up. I believe this is the reason I feel comfortable around diverse cultures.

The name of the ministry GOD gave me is New Wineskin Int'l Ministry, LLC. Luke 5:37&38 says:

> ***And no one puts new wine into old wineskins; or else the new wine will burst the wineskins and be spilled, and the wineskins will be ruined. But new wine must be put into new wineskins, and both are preserved.***

Our mission is to establish the Kingdom of GOD in place of the traditions of men; and impart GOD's Truth to all who will receive, as well as teach people to live supernaturally. Everything we need to live is within us because greater is HE that is within us than he that is in the world (1 John 4:4). GOD has created us in HIS image with the same characteristics. We are creators and have the responsibility to bring heaven into perspective on the earth. The "how" has everything to do with who we are. For some it's singing, others teaching, preaching, playing an instrument, as a bus driver, etc. There are so many diverse ways that GOD uses HIS gifts. My gift as a teacher is what GOD uses to relay his messages "crystal" clear, pun intended.

YOUR TURN

Proverbs 25:2 (TLV)

It is the glory of God to conceal a matter and the glory of kings to search it out.

Thank you for taking the time to read what GOD inspired me to share. Writing this book was harder than birthing five children. I have had to relive some dark places in my life and take a good look at who I was, who I am, and who I choose to become. I bless GOD for walking me through this journey and for angels He assigned to me. The following pages are blank for you to write your story. *Who are you? Why are you here? How did you get there? Where are you going?*

The first time I remember hearing the audible voice of GOD, I was sitting in the Econo

Lodge in Georgia at the table reading the Bible, and I heard a voice saying "come before me." I knew it was the voice of GOD and I went over to the bed and knelt. I said, "Lord, is that you are talking to me?" He replied, "My sheep hear my voice and a stranger they don't hear." I was amazed that GOD was talking to me and I let Him know how in AWE I was and that's when He told me that He is a rewarder of them that diligently seek Him.

The veil is torn giving each one of us direct access to GOD. You don't need anyone to go for you. Over 2000 years ago Jesus' blood paid the price that we couldn't afford. Jesus gave eternal access to ALL who accept in their heart and confess with their mouth that He is Lord. How does that look? Compare it to being at the grocery store, and your bill totals more than you have available.

Instead of you asking the cashier to deduct merchandise, someone comes and pays the price that you couldn't afford, now multiply that by every time you shop!

    How do you respond when someone does something for you? You thank them. We can never pay the price that Jesus paid no matter how hard we work. I referred to DNA in a previous chapter. Our DNA comes from our parents, which carries the record of our ancestral lineage. Jesus' DNA is a record of His parents, which includes both His human and divine record. His Divine nature contains no sin. This is the reason Jesus was the only atonement according to 2 Corinthians 5:21(TLV)

> ***He made the One who knew no sin to become a sin offering on our***

behalf, so that in Him we might become the righteousness of God.

The righteousness of God! That is how important you are. The enemy knows it, and that is the reason why he has been doing everything in his power to prevent you from coming to this point of realization, As Aibileen Clark in the movie, "The Help" says, "You is smart. You is kind. You is important!" You don't have to believe me, ask GOD. He wants to tell you Himself. Where do you start, you ask? Confess and decree it. Say out loud that you have sinned and you accept the work Jesus did by shedding His Blood for you. Don't mumble. Accept responsibility for your sin. Now ask Him to take control of your life and help you surrender it willingly. It's a process, and you may not immediately see results, but you are on the right track. Journaling will help because you can look back and see how far GOD has bought you. Now, ask GOD to show you who HE says you are and why you were born. Start with your name and date of birth. Take your time but get it done. It will change your life.

When The Creator of Everything speaks, you don't always understand with your natural mind; but your spirit comes alive because He is Spirit and the spirit realm is not bound by natural laws. There are things that have been downloaded into my spirit that my natural mind doesn't yet comprehend because there is no point of reference. I know better than to dismiss the information. So I put it on my spiritual shelf until more is revealed. Enjoy getting to know who you are in His eyes. If you need assistance, you can contact New Wineskin

Int'l Ministry at nwimllc@gmail.com. We are here to help you. We will walk alongside you, encourage you and guide you; but we won't do the work for you. This is your process, and it is to your benefit to search it out for yourself.

WHO AM I?

Name and meaning:

_____

_____

_____

_____

_____

Date of Birth and numerical meaning of month and date:

_____

_____

_____

_____

_____

_____

Constellation you were born under:

_____

_____

_____

_____

_____

Why am I here?

You have asked Jesus to take control of your life. Ask Him why you are in your current physical and/or spiritual place. This will require time and maybe even some fasting to hear the answer. Whatever comes to your mind write it down. Don't analyze it.

_____

_____

_____

Crystal Hicks

Crystal Hicks

Crystal Hicks

Crystal Hicks

Crystal Hicks

Crystal Hicks

Crystal Hicks

Crystal Hicks

Crystal Hicks

WHERE AM I GOING?

Habakkuk 2:2 (TLV)

Then *ADONAI* answered me and said:

"Write down the vision,

make it plain on the tablets,

so that the reader may run with it."

Now that you know who GOD says you are and to whom you belong what next? Write down your goals B.C.E (Before Christ's Explanation) and A.C.E (After Christ's Explanation). Submit them to Him and ask for blueprints and strategies that will aid in accomplishing His goals.

_____

_____

_____

Crystal Hicks

Crystal Hicks

Crystal Hicks

Crystal Hicks

Crystal Hicks

AFTERWORD

This would be a good time to invest in your journal. If you are artistic, you may want a journal with no lines so you can draw what GOD is saying to you. If you are more comfortable with writing, then one with lined paper might be a better investment. Whatever way you go, keep track of things you see and hear when you spend time with GOD.

The Lord bless you and watch, guard, and keep you;
The Lord make His face to shine upon and enlighten you and be gracious (kind, merciful, and giving favor) to you;

The Lord lift up His [approving] countenance upon you and give you peace (tranquility of heart and life continually).

(Numbers 6:24-26 AMPC)

www.ingramcontent.com/pod-product-compliance
Lightning Source LLC
Chambersburg PA
CBHW061333040426
42444CB00011B/2906